The Mute

Also by Lars Amund Vaage

In English
Outside the Institution. Selected Poems
Cows, *in* Leopard VI: The Norwegian Feeling for Real

In Norwegian
Poetry
Det andre rommet
Utanfor institusjonen
Den stumme

Fiction
Øvelse kald vinter
Fager kveldssol smiler
Kyr
Dra meg opp!
Baronen
Begynnelsen
Guten med den mjuke magen
Oklahoma
Rubato
Den framande byen. Ein roman om Wilhelm Reich
Guten og den vesle mannen
Kunsten å gå
Tangentane

Translations
Lorine Niedecker: Nord sentralt
Joy Harjo: Å koma tilbake frå fienden
Tennessee Williams: Katt på heitt blekktak
Bob Arnold: Sanndrøymd

Lars Amund Vaage

The Mute

translated by
Kenneth Steven

Shearsman Books

First published in the United Kingdom in 2013 by
Shearsman Books
50 Westons Hill Drive
Emersons Green
BRISTOL
BS16 7DF

Shearsman Books Ltd Registered Office
30–31 St. James Place, Mangotsfield, Bristol BS16 9JB
(this address not for correspondence)

www.shearsman.com

ISBN 978-1-84861-260-0

Acknowledgements
The publisher thanks Forlaget Oktober for permission to publish this
English translation of *Den stumme*.

This translation has been published with the financial support of
NORLA (Norwegian Literature Abroad).

Contents

1.

The Mute

Mute they planted trees on the slopes and let them grow to become
        hissing woods
Mute they came home and the paths opened only to them
Mute they put away their tools in the right places and at the
        right time
Mute they set out the living room floor and carried in the simple
        furnishings
Mute they put out food for the dog, the cat, the hedgehog
Mute they let the milk run in a pattern they had learned in
        another land
Mute they tethered the cows in the byres and stilled their lowing
        mouths
Mute they turned all the buckets and pans, dried them with
        circular motions
Mute they embraced the darkness that came in on them like
        the moors
Mute they cleaned up after eating and let the creatures of the
        wild get the leftovers
Mute they put out plates of pearls for their relatives
Mute they made handles and animal figures that they laid out
        in the grass
Mute they went and sought out subjects for boats and small stories
Mute they gathered up all their years in small bundles they carried
        uppermost on their backs
Mute they greeted when they needed to those they met in their
        dreams
Mute they awoke and turned away from one another
Mute they sat on birthdays and raised glasses from the moments
Mute they waited for the lovers who forgot themselves on the way
        over the mountain lost
Mute they saw the ring glinting on a hand they'd never hold
Mute they warmed a stone that someone should have

The dream melted time
cast me into the moment
I stood in front of the white house
I had heard about its ruination
but it didn't exist
Everything was just as beautifully
tended as before
I didn't go to my own house
the childhood I'd had
once upon a time, but to somewhere else
and searched for the truth
in the doors that opened
and in the hands that sang
I stood motionless
by the gate
No-one was out in the garden
No-one fed the hens
The dog was quiet
The people were not at home
they could have gone
to Paradise or somewhere else
eternal. The house
was emptied
of time
I said:
This is my house
This was my story

I came to the gate, opened it
This was home, a strange place
Among the flowerbeds was white gravel
Black birds sat in the trees
Spruce trees were drawn against the sky
Fish hung from the eaves
The kitchen garden was newly planted
I was inside the fence now
The house was more beautiful than before
My invisible loved ones
were walking across the yard

This house wasn't my home
I see that now
through the thick mist
that's fallen
All the same it is mine
I have had the house cast after me
I see that now
A chance wonder
A joyful warning
It already feels
as though someone has stolen it
back

What's inside the house?
The furniture is collected by relatives
The sun shines through the dirty windows
The floors are worn
The walls shades of green
An impression of that time they sat close together
when I came in

The house rests easy on the earth's edge
In my memory you have soil in your hands
Your hands sink
to the gunnels of the boat that sinks
in the blue Arctic Ocean

The mute shall speak to us
How can that be?
Don't give me body movements or sign language
The mute will speak because he doesn't speak
He chose silence himself
Then it must say everything

The mute one is the wisest
Don't you understand that?
He didn't say the first word
The content got to sleep a long time

The mute one fumbles with his mouth over a new day
He's not just mute, but blind too
His hands search through the hallway and along the kitchen chairs
He can climb onto the wall shelf
and walk under the ceiling beams
He doesn't know where he's going
and therefore he knows

In his heart the mute one
has many sounds he could have shouted

When the mute one speaks at gatherings
he turns away

In my thoughts the mute one runs
not out into the road where cars can hit him
not aimlessly in among the bushes
not over to strangers who come along the road
but rather he runs to me

The mute one gets up silently
He eats four eggs and a bowl of porridge before he goes out into
        the springtime
that green, green morning is also silent
He goes out of the house I still don't know is mine
He has nothing with him because he doesn't know he'll go
The mute one stands naked where one day I will stand
He is grey and see-through as the morning mist
His tools lie in a secret pattern on the workbench
The bowl of milk is in the cupboard
The buckets hang upside down from the drying stand
The horse he's let out to graze, but he has no memory of it
The cows stand tethered in their stalls, satisfied
Everything is as usual
Nothing is as before
Remains of invisible bodies lie in the furrows
Traces of the ancestors are rubbed away
The work that's done is hidden in the woods
In the outhouse lie ploughs for horses
On the slate roof the moss grows thick and wet
Along the roadsides the grass is clipped short
Nothing pushes up from the new-sown meadows
The walls aren't visible at the boundaries
The boat's drawn up into the boathouse, right up to the big rock
Soundlessly it turns over on its side
The prow feels good to the touch but no-one knows
The oak trees along the roadside stand leafless
The dew lies in the gravel track
The mute one has forgotten

There came a mute friend to the mute one
rowing across the fiord
He cast to one side the stones on the shore
and dragged his boat up into the grass
He came up the sea road
and in to the yard
He opened the door without knocking
and breathed new colours
which in reality were the old ones
on the walls of the kitchen and the living room
They sat down in front of the television
and mimed all the programmes
until the evening news was over
Then they sat there a long while
thinking of that time
they ran with their arms by their sides
all the way from the grey boathouse
to the shores of America

The mute one left for his work on the land
He went out the door and down the stone steps
out onto the path to the garden gate. The worm
had crept halfway across. The mute one
went on along the main road, then
made his way into the wood
to the little valley where the ones of old
had washed themselves
in the spring that was now full of muck, but
where the walls of it still stood. One day
he'd clean the spring
throw the dirt up onto the sides
he thought; the women would come again
to the well with their washing
even though washing machines had been introduced
He went further still into the larch wood
could glimpse the road a bit away
The trees changed places and fell
in the corner of his eye
He went right in to the lumber wood
found the axe that lay hidden in the nest
he'd built of leaves and branches
There he also had
the saw
the wedge
the measure for wood
and a soft stone

Go to the toolbox
That could be his grave
Go to it if it exists
and lives somewhere in the darkness
Go to such as do not exist
in it
Square rules, planes and a rod for measuring
Go to the axes that once were
and ask about the journeys
and the world on the other side

The toolbox stands in the half-dark of the outhouse
Dust lies over the workbench and the floorboards
Shavings lie in a corner, will soon return to soil
The toolbox whispers with its hard, rough tongue
The toolbox received the gift of speech and
the sharp square rules, the knives, the saws
There was a time the planes howled
across white wood
The rasps warned of evening
There are feet round the toolbox
They stand, they go
The mute one wanders
with the toolbox
His feet are in the box and the box
is in his feet
There were times
he threw the axe over his shoulder
and went towards the building he should construct
or the gunnel of a boat
He got close to the tree
he should fell, and carry
to the point of the journey between
the parts of the world. He saw
the building coming towards him
or was it he
that went closer?
He gripped hammer and saw
forced the wood into the walls
bound the bars together
with open spaces. He
felt the burning
in his hard hands
when he made love

The sailing ship towed time in towards the horizon
Its wake rubbed out the lips. The mute one
put his arms round the dead toolbox
He had to keep himself awake even though
night and day were the same, his eyes
saw only dark blue
He sharpened the knives, alone
near the bottom of the boat. And so he worked
wood into wood, mast into mast
He mixed strength into the boards
so the storm stilled

Come with me up the road to the white house
Hear the mute birdsong
It's a still summer morning
All you need is a small pair of trousers on your child's frame
Sense the morning air, cold against the skin
sharp gravel underfoot
But it'll soon be warmer
and your skin underfoot thicker
Come with me to work
The haymaking's about to start and the mute one's
waiting for us. Come on the road to his kingdom
He's got out the scythe
Bacon rind lies under the axle of the whetstone
It's my job to turn the stone
for him. Now the steel whines
against the round stone
and the water splashes in the trough
How many times must I turn
the stone, I ask

He sits in new-cut grass
I see the polished crown of his head
a fly creeps into his furrows
I am with him or beside him
He gets up
He's no tall man
He swings the scythe on the steep slope
That's how to do it, he says
Turn the edge a little up
so it won't hit a stone

He sits in the grass
It's a new summer
It's me that swings the scythe now
He can't manage any more
My feet won't, he says
But I'm young and fit and pile
the grass in under his pear trees
Soon I'll go
to the other youngsters

It's a new spring and a new summer
We should have had the boat out
But she lies cracking in the boathouse
It's yet another new spring and a new autumn
And the pears are lying in the tall grass
rotting
he says

Just make your gifts here, he said
and threw out his hands, for I'd asked
if I could use his work place for Christmas presents
Before he went, he pointed to the toolbox
the grinding saws, the work bench
with the two screw vices
the wood to be crafted that hung on the wall
half-finished axe-shafts made of ash, something
which was to make a rocker, a baler,
oars, rough-hewn
I still stood alone
and gripped
down into the dark
for tools

Work came before the word
Work was the word
And the word put the land under its authority
The looking after of animals came first
The mute one delivered them
swept the mucous from their mouths
with his hands
and put them to their mothers
so that she could lick them
Hay and silage came before the word
The wood came before the word
The woods stood waiting
for whose who still weren't born
The unborn came before the word
The unborn guide our steps
when we go off to work
The stone walls came before the word
The stone walls said their piece
a long time ago
They were quieter than the night
The fishing trips came before the word
The mute one sat in the back of the boat
had the net in his lap
before he let it out
That was before the word
The measuring bucket and the ladders and the slates
and the fence posts and the vegetable fields
came before the word
The ditches came before the word
Long before I was born
The mute one dug ditches in the big sump
He put

earth from it onto one side
and stones and roots on the other
He dug till he couldn't lift the spade
He dug till his back was bent
and his fingers couldn't let go of the handle
All this was before the word
He put stones in all the ditches
and spread earth over them again
Silent the stones lay
in the black earth
Many years passed
The ditches drained the sump
waterless, made of it
the best of meadows
That was before the word

They had no children
I came to them instead. They
gave birth to me one afternoon
Right away I could talk
My words
were tepid water
over bright wood
They made room for me lightning quick
somewhere in the house
I will never forget
the words they could have spoken

One time when I came
to them, I was shown in
to the beautiful room
where the furniture
stood untouched. I sat
alone there a while
They came
with the best food
warm drink, the cakes
that I loved so
But I would rather
have been out with them
in the kitchen and hovering
in that still mumbling

That's how to do it, he said
and put water on the fastening
which held the scythe to its shaft
That's how to do it, he said
another time
and gave me the knife
so I could sharpen
and he'd do the turning
That's how to do it, he repeated
and we went together
along the red walls
that he had built
It was evening
we came to the stone walls
that divide the land
in two. That's
how to do it
he said, and laid his head
against my chest

I wanted to work too, not for meaning
but outside all meaning

I wanted to work like you, not for income or honour
but for another law that governs creation

I wanted to work so that the stones in the scree were laid in the
        right place

I wanted to work faithfully, blind, so that thought would leave me
That would be my only meaning

I wanted to work so my heart would beat faster yet regularly
And my heart would beat on towards eternal rest

I wanted to work constantly and calmly, put stress on the breaks
never hurry on to evening

Freedom, freedom, freedom—I would never coerce you
but let you remain lying on flat stones

I would hold the tools lightly, not cling to the handle
I would swing the hammer and the axe so that I'd disappear

Who was mother?
I didn't know
before the mute ones
had wandered
from the house
to the tall
grass at the edge of the beyond

I saw mother standing
where she'd always been
in the light
among the cupboard doors
that waved her onwards

I found her
in the deep fields
on the abandoned farms
where the livestock
had passed into dreams

One day I saw her coming
out into the yard
On the green plain
she bent down
and formed words
to the grass

She sat by the baking table that hovered away
She took her rolling pin over cake heaven
The baking table stood in a smoke of flour
and the wood that burned in the open grate
I came into the low, grey cellar
stood for a time before I knew
that I could run
for more wood
that was the task I'd been given
by she who sat
with warmth on the one side
and cold on the other
I fetched the fine wood
from the shed
Sprang across the yard
with the fresh air in my lungs
and the taste of new-baked cake in my mouth
sprang and sprang to a secret place

Mother was finished with the baking
She used many movements
to explain something
I didn't understand

She cooled the cakes
and put them in the cupboard while she talked to me
about what she didn't say

She was free after doing the baking
hurried
over the worn floor

Enfolded me
in her sweaty dress

Day in night
Day in dream
Just opened themselves
of inner light
How could air be
silk one did not see
and floorboards carry crying
over the black ridge

You woman who carried
your ripened womb
out into the grey evening
that was like wet wood

You carried also your pointed
heavy breasts
right down to the sea
where the seaweed waited

You went further
Waded over the muddy floor
didn't stop at the hill crest
Let the child out
in the fishes' heaven

2.

Songs of Death and Love

The boat is no longer in the boathouse
But out on the water somewhere
It goes the length of beaches
and passes steep rocks
soon it's far out on the fiord
The boat works with time
dividing it into moments
that do not hang together
Remains of waves come
to deserted bays
One day the keel drives
into land on the other side

The boat carries you over the water
You are her gift to the horizon
The water carries the boat with its mouth
kisses and lifts her, up to the wind

One day the water muscle will break
The will of the water will dissolve
into cold falls

Then the boat will fly over the water heaven
She will dance in an undersea wind
towards the upside down horizon

You don't sit safe in a boat
It can break
when the water opens
The water has mouths like black suns
and you must think:
I came here
Life is over
I forgot time
The way went along the woods
In groups of houses the bonfire burned
under the cooking pots
The food came on tongues
Sleep stroked your bare skin

In autumn the boat has to come in to the boatshed
She rises slowly from the water
and comes in to the half-dark
She towers over the concrete floor
stands untouched and thinks
Her fish heart is under the bottom boards
There lies a little blood
and a rusted knife

People will guard the boat
Polish her, oil her base
keep her clean
They'll close the doors on the winter storms
go further inland
and wait

On the bright beach you can find
the old boathouse
Master builders kept it in condition for a thousand years
replaced stones
exchanged rotten posts

Inside the boathouse lie the old boats
reminders of hands
or the hip-curves of women
Boats that twisted in the water
make the journey still
from wood to dust

The oldest boat lies
deep in a bog
Remains of skin stretched
over its frame like the skin of the face
of some old soul
A little boy thought
of this boat
when he ran
with a bark boat in his hands
over a stony bit of ground

There was a long way still to go
hadn't noticed that night was falling
A voice said to me
that I had arrived
They led me in
to a grey beach
an empty sky
I made no protest
I turned and saw
a new past
I didn't know
that my work shone
of fortune
or that life with you
was the greatest thing of all

I went in to the dark valley
I came as far as that place
the ferryman waited. I saw his face
when I turned
and went home
Not long after
came God's hand
and gave me forgetfulness
He sent me out into life again
so that I would know
the same fear as before
It's best that way
he said

What is it like in the house of the fisherman when he comes
        home in the evening?
He's been out the whole day at sea in the wind and the waves
Afterwards he gutted the fish and weighed them
Then he made fast the boat and rowed to land
What is it like in the house of the fisherman when he comes
        home in the evening?
Sometimes the house lies still in darkness
His wife has gone to bed and the lights are out
and there's no-one to meet him in the hall
No-one takes his clothes when he pulls them off
What is it like in the house of the fisherman when he comes
        home in the evening?
Sometimes there's light in the kitchen
When his wife hears steps, she opens the door for him
She takes the fish he'd brought home for dinner
She lifts his hands to the light and says:
Oh, if only you could find peace here with me

Early in the morning the fisherman had to go out to the fishing
        grounds
He climbed down the ladder from the jetty because it was low tide
and rowed out to the boat that lay moored
When the signal came he was ready

He fished the whole day on the restless sea
The fish flopped in over the side
The boat was thrown this way and that by the quick waves
but the fisherman kept on his feet

In the evening the sea rose up over the edge of the jetty
The fisherman went home to the still, dark house
Barefoot he stole over the slippery floor
for he mustn't disturb those who were sleeping

The fisherman mourned the sea
that dragged itself back
to a distant place
His children ran
over the white sea floor

He sorrowed over the woman
he could see
but not know
when they went together
through the deserted harbours

He sorrowed over the words
he had seen coming
in his own mouth

But most of all he sorrowed
over the glad laughter
he'd had on his tongue
when he met people at sea

Coyly the explosives' workers bow themselves to humanity
cautiously they share their wisdom, gentle
from all the explosions in the bedrock

Over the explosives' workers there lies a layer
of dust while they bore the plots
The rock dust makes their hair stiff
and their skin soft as silk
Their lips red

The explosives' workers stand in noise, support
themselves to the boring rigs. The explosives' workers sleep
in the grey clouds that rise
from the earth's birth

The explosives' workers call when the salvos are to go off
Their voice sounds and they run this way and that, calling upon
all those who need to get out of the way

The explosives' workers stand out in the mauve
evening light, a foot up on the running board
of dirty lorries. They have hands
bent for the scooping of baptismal water. Now
they sing, child soprano voices

When the explosives workers die they are crushed
between machinery and blocks of rock that
meet in screes where there come small puffs of smoke
from the edges that resemble
the dust from drilling. The evening
does not notice

The moon watches over the town tonight
We sit in the warm darkness of the café
Outside it's winter, the same, in an army of others
The fire burns in the grate and cracks in the walls
The dark windows reflect us, I see
your hips, hidden in mist
your mouth breaks into smiling
your hands live on both sides
of the plate, your words give me answers
and forgetfulness
even though you just come out
with the usual sentences
I won't go
to the party haunts where reports of the mood
threaten to drown out fortune
I will sit here as long as time
is still and lives in you
You get up, we go
now we are outside
in the same winter
don't know
where we will go

I look at the things you brought that day not long ago
You put the irreplaceable up on shelves, cupboards and small tables
an inherited piece of jewellery, gifts from your school days, books
about other countries
You didn't need to push anything of mine to one side since there
was plenty of room

Your things were colours or hopes
Your things were sunlight or cool water
Your things breathed riddles or a future into my own
Now the decoration hovers over the edges of the living room
when you come near

Still you remain in the house you built that first evening
You made a room that I couldn't leave
On occasion I forgot where I was
You didn't know my story of apple twigs and green mornings

Still I see you every day in the midst of the night sky
I see you coming from the bathroom at peace with yourself and
            with wheels of time
I see your happiness lying under your skin, forgotten for a few hours
Who gave you the calm steps and the silent dance?

You couldn't know where I came from and what lived in my heart
I said nothing to anyone because it was forbidden me
I didn't start the days with song and take you in my arms
I didn't talk to you because I shut words out of your house

All the same you waited for me each evening by the rest stone
When I came walking to the old place, you were always there
How could you give me the riddle that you loved me?

Each day we go for walks with the dog
She springs in among the trees
wild with joy over cones
twigs and scents from the hummocks

We walk unknown paths
don't know what will meet us
at the next viewpoint
The whole world
is forest

It's the middle of the day
Ages ago you sent the kids on their way to school
In their bags they had
their jotters with rugged handwriting
Now they sit in front of blackboards of knowledge
in the room where the clock stands still
The sun is high in the sky
Hear the cars out in the street
They're not driving out from their morning gates
neither are they going home for supper
but gore their way
to something unfinished
There is a moment that splits the day
After lunch the poem resumes
It's too late to begin a new text
too much has been said
too many thoughts written down
To be able to go on is the richest gift
In the afternoon hours the poem is finished
But mornings will return
the frail grey light rise again
and you will meet your loved ones
by the breakfast table

The summer lay worn out around us
The morning was still grey
We went and searched for cafés
Houses fell down and rose up in the place where we walked
The leaves withered and grew anew on the lilacs
The air bit my throat when you said:
We are together

You knew me as I was not
You saw passed what I said and did
in to a red point
where the eye met fruit
of birth and hope

You saw the person I was not
You knew the word behind the word
and the laughter was another man
rejoicing over something
no-one had seen

You freed me from the fate
that had formed me
My tongue unfolded
in the light from your mouth
My hands could play
on an invisible keyboard

Be glad that you will perhaps betray me
The flowers and the trees around me have said this to me
The summer clouds have told me of it
Now I go silent and lightly clad
through the forest that you showed me

Be happy that the time we have together will soon be finished
Be glad for the sorrow lurking somewhere in the house
Be glad for all that will be taken from us
together with the memory of that which was

Don't complain about the passing of time
Each hour that's over greets us from the other side
Each deserted second builds a richness in the body
Each forgotten caress
opens the room anew

We went together out into the day
We went through the flowering forest
That opened to the vast moorlands of sea and stone

We went under the endless sky
Where the years chased through us like rain and wind
And there came high days, low sun
And beautiful meetings with these closest

We went through dark corridors in the ugliest of houses
Right to the border posts by a fast-flowing river
We came to the place
Where our legs couldn't carry us
And our hearts perhaps would not beat

We were torn from each other by sense and hope
I took off all my clothes and the ring I had received from you
I gave myself up to that sleep
dreams did not haunt

When I woke up you were there, crying and laughing
You took my hand and we went towards the light
of the parking lot. I looked
at my hands and every surface:

My trouser legs, the windscreen. The fjord sky
we rushed through

Your breath
supported me on the steep road
in to the seating
and the testimony to the days
we had had
A pencil stub lay
where I'd left it
I could write
what I saw

The Author

Lars Amund Vaage was born in 1952 in Sunde on the west coast of Norway. He studied the piano and later literature at the University of Bergen. Since 1979 he has published eleven novels, one book of short stories, three collections of poetry and a play, children's books and several translations, including works by Lorine Niedecker and Joy Harjo. Vaage has received many awards, among them the Brage Prize 2012 for his latest novel *Syngja* (Sing), the Aschehoug Publisher's prize for his novel *Rubato* (1995) for which he was also nominated for the Nordic Council literary award. He received the Dobloug prize from the Swedish Academy (1997), the Gyldendal Publisher's prize (2002), the Radio Listeners' prize for his novel *Kunsten å gå* (The Art of Walking) and the Emmaus Prize in 2005 for his novel *Tangentane* (The Piano Keys)—among several others. His novel about the Jewish psychiatrist Wilhelm Reich's time in Norway, *Den framande byen* (The Strange City, 1999), caused quite a debate. *Syngja*, about a father and his autistic daughter, about writing and speechlessness, has touched many readers. His work has appeared in German, Russian, Hindi, Polish and English. He is considered one of the most original and accomplished writers of his generation.

Among its reasons for giving the award, the jury for the Aschehoug prize said that Vaage was an "unusually refined literary artist, sensuously symbolic, concrete and succinct, and with something as rare as a loving irony".

"an extremely elegant, wise and challenging storyteller"
—Stavanger Aftenblad

The Translator

Kenneth Steven was born in Glasgow in 1968 but moved to Highland Perthshire during his schooldays. He has studied and taught in Norway, and translated from both Norwegian and Sami.

A widely published poet, novelist and children's author, his collections of poems include *A Song Among the Stones* (2012), *Evensong* (2011), *Island: Collected Poems* (2009), *Making the Known World New* (2009), and *Iona* (2000). His translation of Lars Saaybe Christensen's *Half Brother* was a finalist for the 2004 Independent Foreign Fiction Prize.

www.ingramcontent.com/pod-product-compliance
Lightning Source LLC
Chambersburg PA
CBHW031932080426
42734CB00007B/649